GEOLOGY GENIUS
IGNEOUS ROCKS

by Rebecca Pettiford

Ideas for Parents and Teachers

Pogo Books let children practice reading informational text while introducing them to nonfiction features such as headings, labels, sidebars, maps, and diagrams, as well as a table of contents, glossary, and index.

Carefully leveled text with a strong photo match offers early fluent readers the support they need to succeed.

Before Reading

- "Walk" through the book and point out the various nonfiction features. Ask the student what purpose each feature serves.
- Look at the glossary together. Read and discuss the words.

Read the Book

- Have the child read the book independently.
- Invite him or her to list questions that arise from reading.

After Reading

- Discuss the child's questions. Talk about how he or she might find answers to those questions.
- Prompt the child to think more. Ask: Have you ever been near a volcano? Did you notice igneous rock in the area?

Pogo Books are published by Jump!
5357 Penn Avenue South
Minneapolis, MN 55419
www.jumplibrary.com

Copyright © 2019 Jump!
International copyright reserved in all countries.
No part of this book may be reproduced in any form without written permission from the publisher.

Library of Congress Cataloging-in-Publication Data

Names: Pettiford, Rebecca, author.
Title: Igneous rocks / by Rebecca Pettiford.
Description: Minneapolis, MN: Jump!, Inc., [2018]
Series: Geology genius | Audience: Ages 7-10.
Includes index.
Identifiers: LCCN 2017054180 (print)
LCCN 2017057867 (ebook)
ISBN 9781624968358 (ebook)
ISBN 9781624968334 (hardcover: alk. paper)
ISBN 9781624968341 (pbk.)
Subjects: LCSH: Igneous rocks—Juvenile literature.
Classification: LCC QE461 (ebook)
LCC QE461 .P485 2018 (print) | DDC 552/.1—dc23
LC record available at https://lccn.loc.gov/2017054180

Editor: Kristine Spanier
Book Designer: Michelle Sonnek
Content Consultant: Sandra Feher, M.S.G.E.

Photo Credits: All photos by Shutterstock.

Printed in the United States of America at Corporate Graphics in North Mankato, Minnesota.

TABLE OF CONTENTS

CHAPTER 1
Igneous Rock Formation 4

CHAPTER 2
Intrusive and Extrusive 10

CHAPTER 3
In Our Daily Lives 18

ACTIVITIES & TOOLS
Try This! 22
Glossary 23
Index 24
To Learn More 24

CHAPTER 1
IGNEOUS ROCK FORMATION

Earth is always changing. Old rock breaks down. New rock forms. This is called the **rock cycle**.

Igneous is one type of rock on Earth. There are two more. **Sedimentary** and **metamorphic**. How does igneous rock form?

igneous rock

CHAPTER 1   5

Earth's crust is made of **plates**. They are always shifting. **Magma** is underneath. This is hot, melted rock. It is so hot that it feels like fire!

TAKE A LOOK!

Earth's plates shift and move. Rock is always being recycled.

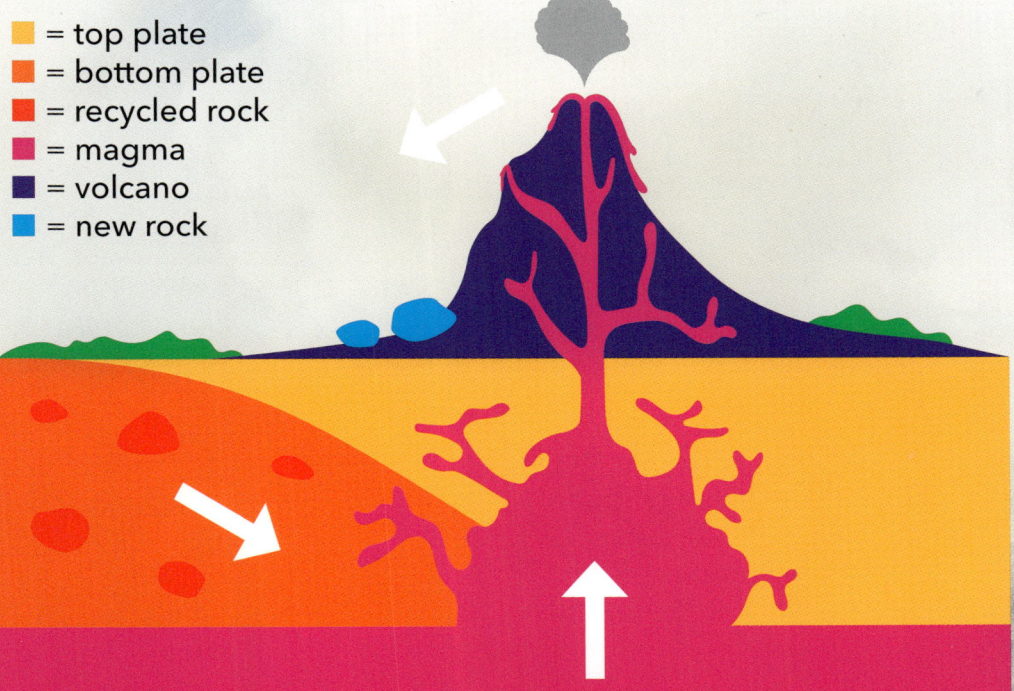

- ▇ = top plate
- ▇ = bottom plate
- ▇ = recycled rock
- ▇ = magma
- ▇ = volcano
- ▇ = new rock

CHAPTER 1

Igneous rock forms when magma cools. Sometimes it cools under Earth's surface. It cools above Earth's surface, too. How? When **volcanoes** erupt, magma turns into **lava**. It cools and hardens. This is igneous rock.

> **DID YOU KNOW?**
>
> An active volcano is one that has had at least one eruption in the past 10,000 years. There are more than 1,500 active volcanoes in the world!

CHAPTER 1

CHAPTER 2
INTRUSIVE AND EXTRUSIVE

There are two types of igneous rock. One is called **intrusive**. It forms under the surface of Earth. The magma cools slowly. Over time, it hardens into rock. Devils Tower is an example. Softer rock **eroded** around it. The igneous rock still stands.

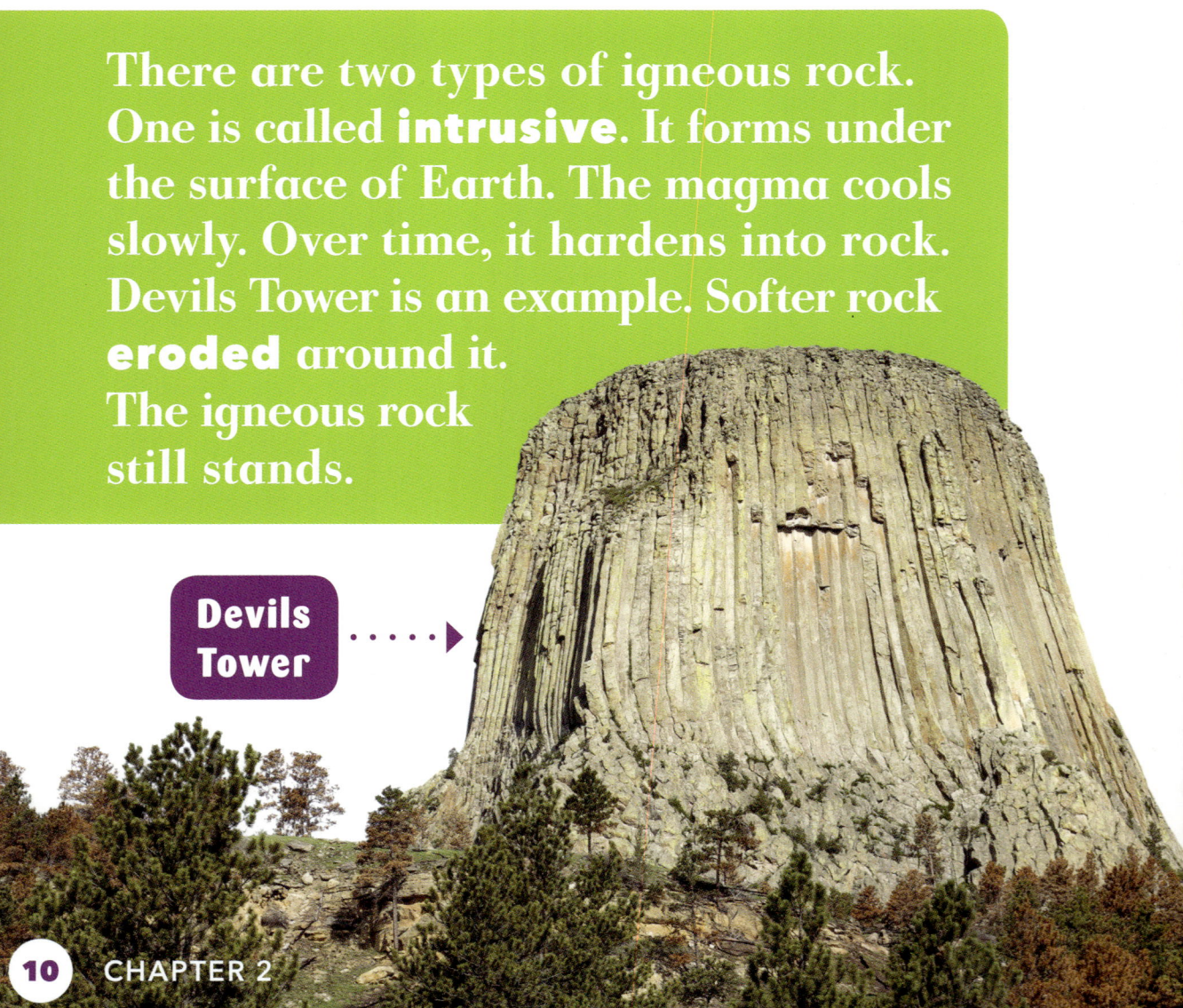

Devils Tower

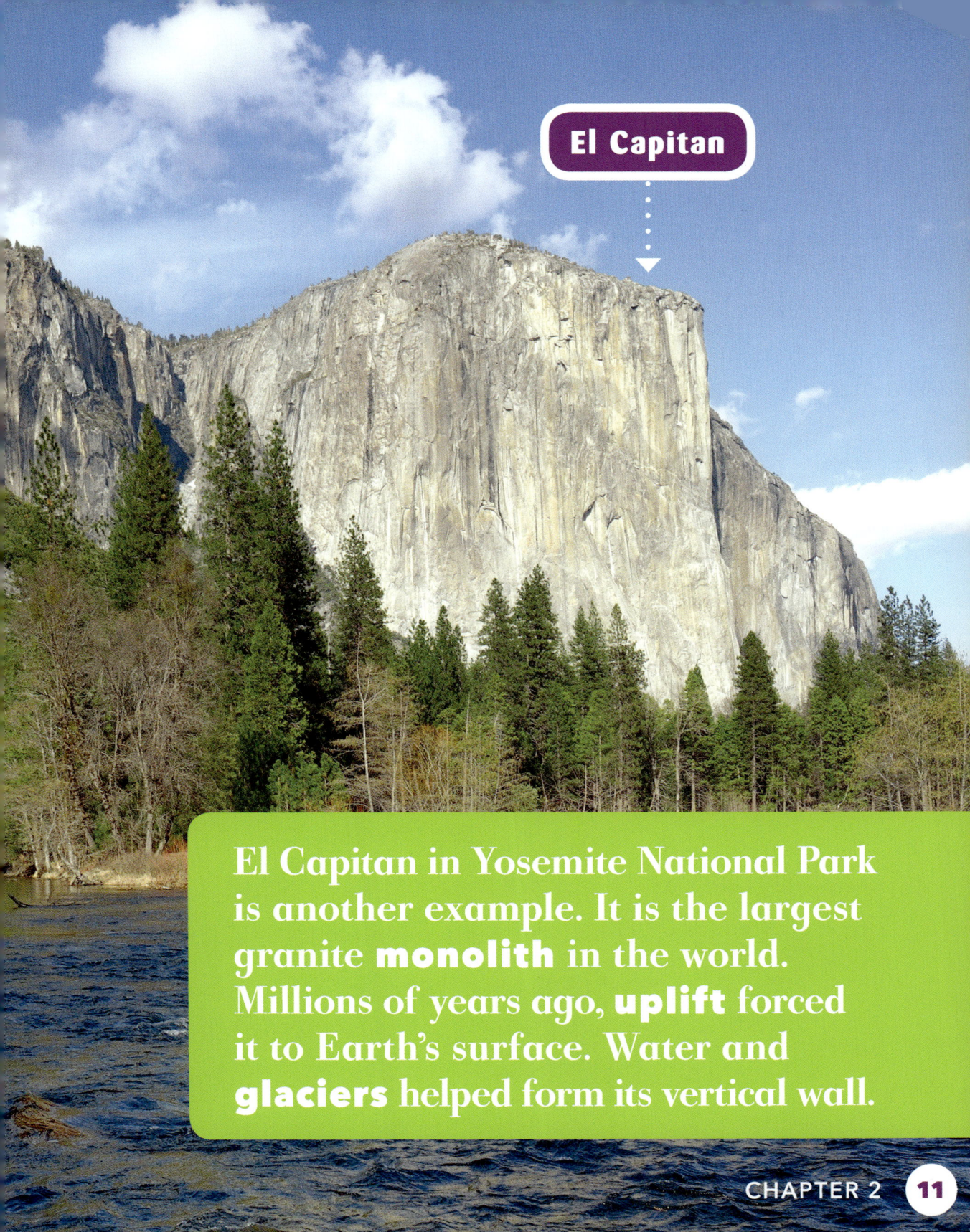

El Capitan

El Capitan in Yosemite National Park is another example. It is the largest granite **monolith** in the world. Millions of years ago, **uplift** forced it to Earth's surface. Water and **glaciers** helped form its vertical wall.

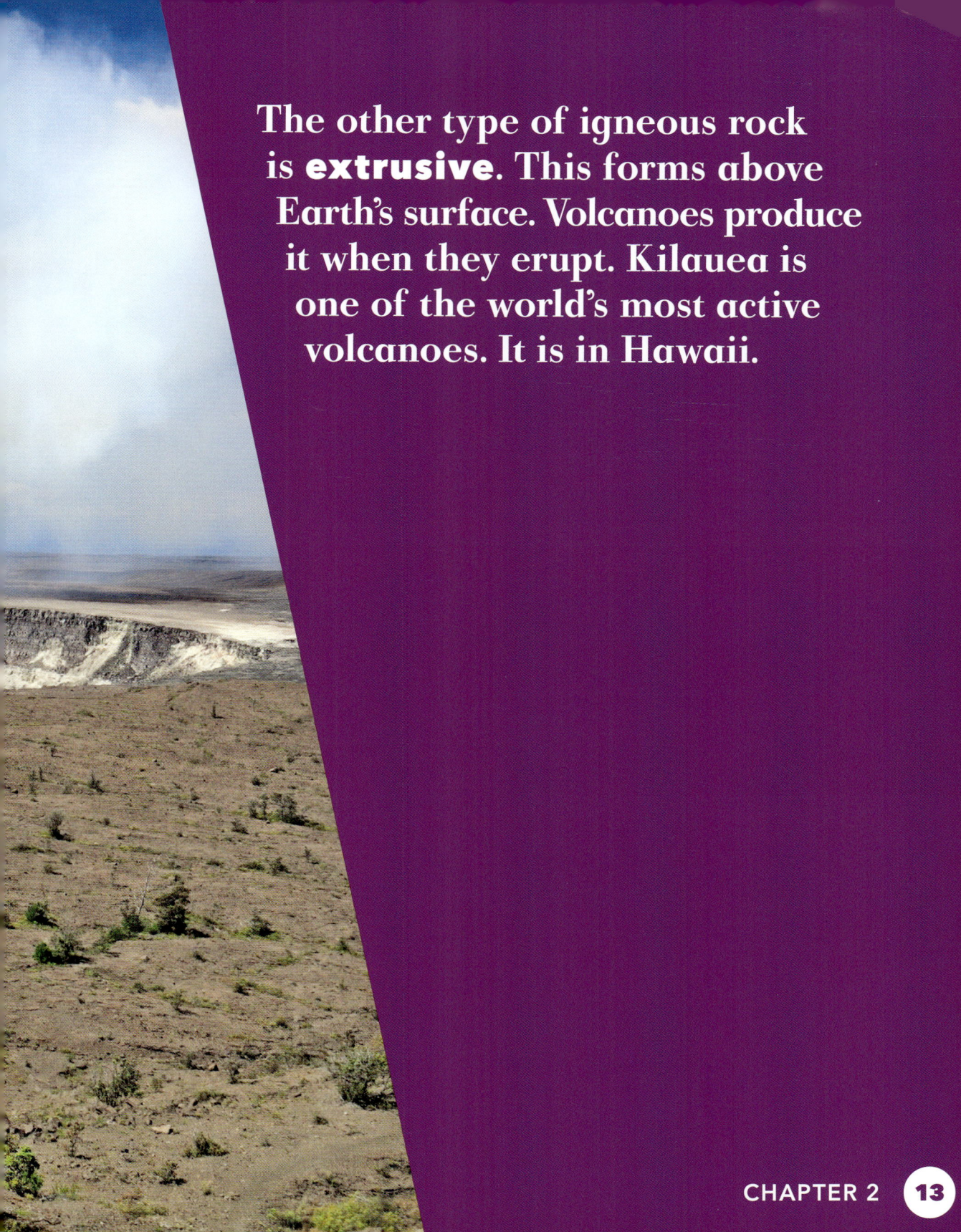

The other type of igneous rock is **extrusive**. This forms above Earth's surface. Volcanoes produce it when they erupt. Kilauea is one of the world's most active volcanoes. It is in Hawaii.

Hawaii has a green sand beach. Why? Olivine **crystals** formed as magma cooled under Earth. This became rock on the surface. Water erodes the rock. It turns into green sand. Many people visit this special beach every day.

DID YOU KNOW?

Volcanoes can make lava tubes. What are they? Tunnels made of igneous rock. As the lava flows, it cools. The sides of the flow crust over. This forms a roof. Some tubes are as big as subway tunnels!

◀······ green sand

CHAPTER 2 15

Giant's Causeway is in Ireland. It has more than 40,000 basalt columns. Lava formed them more than 50 million years ago. The columns look like big stepping stones. Some are 39 feet (12 meters) tall!

CHAPTER 3

IN OUR DAILY LIVES

> How do we use igneous rock?
> We build monuments with granite.

It is also used in buildings. Some people have granite in their homes.

granite

We can use pumice to make our skin soft. It is also used in some toothpastes. It has holes in it. The holes make it light. It can float in water!

Look around. What kind of igneous rock do you see every day?

DID YOU KNOW?

Why does pumice have holes in it? Lava comes into contact with cold water. Rapid cooling creates gas bubbles. The holes are left behind.

ACTIVITIES & TOOLS

TRY THIS!

SINKING AND RISING LIQUIDS

Try this activity to see how the density of a substance affects its movement.

What You Need:
- mason jar or drinking glass
- 1 cup of room temperature water
- food coloring
- ¼ cup vegetable oil
- 1 teaspoon salt (coarse rock salt is good)

❶ **Add water to mason jar.**

❷ **Add four or five drops of food coloring and stir.**

❸ **Add oil to the jar.**

❹ **Sprinkle salt into the mixture. What do you notice?**

The oil floats on top because it is less dense than the water. Salt captures some oil as it sinks. As the salt dissolves, it releases the oil. The oil then rises again. The difference in density between the oil and water is the same process in which magma rises to the surface. It is less dense than the surrounding rock. Uplift from Earth's plates shifting will also force igneous rock to the surface.

GLOSSARY

crystals: Repeating, three-dimensional arrangements of atoms or molecules.

eroded: Worn away by water, wind, heat, or ice.

extrusive: Igneous rock that forms above Earth's surface.

glaciers: Slow-moving ice masses.

intrusive: Igneous rock that forms below Earth's surface.

lava: Hot, liquid rock that pours out of fissures or an erupting volcano.

magma: Melted rock beneath Earth's surface that becomes lava when it flows out of volcanoes and fissures.

metamorphic: Of or having to do with rock that has been transformed by pressure or heat.

monolith: A single great stone often in the form of an obelisk or column.

plates: The flat, rigid, rocky pieces that make up Earth's outer crust.

rock cycle: The continuous process by which rocks are created, changed from one form to another, destroyed, and then formed again.

sedimentary: Rock that is formed by layers of sediment that have been pressed together.

uplift: To cause a portion of Earth's surface to rise above adjacent areas.

volcanoes: Mountains with openings through which molten lava, ash, and hot gases erupt.

ACTIVITIES & TOOLS

INDEX

basalt columns 17
Devils Tower 10
El Capitan 11
eroded 10, 14
extrusive 13
Giant's Causeway 17
granite 11, 18, 19
intrusive 10
Kilauea 13
lava 8, 14, 17, 21
lava tubes 14

magma 6, 7, 8, 10, 14
metamorphic 5
monolith 11
olivine crystals 14
plates 6, 7
pumice 21
rock cycle 4
sedimentary 5
uplift 11
volcanoes 7, 8, 13
water 11, 14, 21

TO LEARN MORE

Learning more is as easy as 1, 2, 3.
1) Go to www.factsurfer.com
2) Enter "igneousrocks" into the search box.
3) Click the "Surf" button to see a list of websites.

With factsurfer, finding more information is just a click away.